D0731901

When Bosses Go Wild

Preventing Employee Morale Knockouts

Eddie Loussararian

Dedication

This book is dedicated to my beautiful wife, Michelle, who read every word of every line of every draft I produced and helped me stay focused on completing my book. She is my rock and I am forever humbled in her presence. When I look in the mirror, I see her reflection staring back at me. I will always be enraptured by her love.

Special thanks to Allen Analian for cover editing

Allen Productions / Engineering, www.allen.dj

For training seminars or information about *When Bosses Go Wild*

Email: eloussararian@yahoo.com

"If you talk to a man in a language he understands, that goes to his head. If you talk to a man in a language he knows, it goes to his heart."

—Nelson Mandela

Contents

Acknowledgements

I would like to thank God for putting the desire in my heart and for giving me the ability to write this book.

"What then shall we say to these things? If God is for us, who can be against us?"

—Romans 8:31

I am grateful to my many friends and colleagues who took time from their busy schedules to review this manuscript and provide their feedback.

I would also like to thank the powerful leaders that played an instrumental role in the formative years of my life. My Mother, Mary, has been a constant source of encouragement throughout my life. She has imparted her passion for life and the Lord within us. And to my Father, John, who sacrificed so much to ensure I obtained a great education, and put me to work at a young age to instill his strong work ethic.

Professionally, I would like to thank Tim Nare, who was my first boss out of college. Tim taught me the finer points of setting clear expectations and holding team members and myself accountable. Omar Janjua, who was my first mentor, honed my time management skills and encouraged me to look at problems with a critical eye. And finally, to Richard Demeter, my High School English Teacher, who spent countless hours of his own time developing my writing skills. I will always be indebted for the investment he made in my life.

Finally, I would like to thank my children for exercising patience while I spent countless hours giving life to my thoughts and emotions. As you grow up, let this be yet another reason to be proud of your Father. Your Mother and I have been working tirelessly to raise you in the presence of our Lord and guide you through this thing called life. I love you Shant, Tatiana, and Marie.

Introduction:
Preventing Employee Morale Knockouts

When Bosses Go Wild is written with the belief that employees and supervisors can peacefully co-exist without destroying employee morale. For years, there has been a power struggle between the two combatants to improve such things as productivity, organizational culture, and working conditions.

Despite countless books, videos, and training seminars available today, a noticeable chasm still exists as it has for decades.

Whether in technology, hospitality, or manufacturing, the role of a manager is to get work done through others. Effective managers navigate through the four functions of management: planning, organizing, leading, and controlling, but sometimes fall short of the softer side of the game: motivating, encouraging, recognizing, and inspiring their employees to willingly go beyond the call of duty.

Managers have an unmistakably difficult road to plow as they strive to meet company objectives. They are tasked with improving workflows, increasing sales, margin, productivity, quality, and service. The challenge for supervisors is that they can seldom accomplish their goals without involving their subordinates. Whether through directing or delegating the activities of their teams, managers are confounded by selecting the right people to complete tasks while injecting a high dose of motivation into team members.

When the leader, the follower, and the situation are aligned, not only will the project succeed, but employee morale will be positively impacted. Another way to look at this is that managers need to make a connection with employees to identify the best way to lead them. Although becoming 'buddies' is not recommended, at the very least, supervisors should know something about their employee's spouse, children, or hobbies. That way, they can show sympathy and care if the opportunity presents itself.

According to an independent study conducted by the Author, 87% of working students between the ages of 21 – 50 stated that they appreciated it when their boss asked about their children. They went on to say that it was that connection that made working longer hours and dealing with challenging situations more tolerable.

As compared to their supervisors, employees have different expectations for work. Aside from the need to earn a fair wage, workers want to work in a well-run, fun-loving, productive environment that encourages creativity and recognizes hard work and results. According to an employee survey, 42% of respondents stated that their morale was negatively affected when their boss failed to recognize them for – what they felt – was a job well done. Those employees went on to say that, although the company's culture played a role in their enthusiasm, when their supervisor failed to say, "Thank you" after the completion of a project, it made them second-guess whether their work was appreciated.

This book will attempt to answer the age-old question employees ask about their boss: "Why does my Manager treat me this way?" Although this Author is grateful for all of the positive role models he has had over his career and, by no means, intends to cast a negative shadow over caring supervisors who go out of their way to create a positive work environment, this book will focus on bad bosses that make the workplace so unpleasant that employees have to give serious thought about seeking greener pastures elsewhere.

Each morale killer, referred to a "round", is dedicated to a management problem as seen through the eyes of employees and is followed by recommendations for both employees and managers. If you have experienced any of the scenarios outlined in this book, the Author empathizes with you and wants you to know that you are not alone. Fear not! We will get through this together.

Round 1: The Skeptic

Problem

Ronald Reagan used to tell a story of two brothers: an optimist and a pessimist. In the optimist's room, there was a mound of manure, while in the pessimist's room, there was a pile of toys. One day, the parents went into the pessimist's room and found him crying. He thought all those toys were too good to be true and was waiting for someone to take them away from him.

The optimist, on the other hand, was feverishly digging through the manure when his parents walked into the room. The boy said, "With all this manure, there's bound to be a pony in here somewhere."

Is your boss an optimist or a pessimist? Does he look at the glass as half full or half empty? Does your supervisor assume you are busy doing other things besides working on your assigned projects? Has your boss ever called your office phone and then seconds later your cell phone because you did not answer the first call fast enough? Has one of your co-workers walked up to you to let you know that your boss was looking for you?

If so, sorry you had to deal with that, but you're not alone.

Why do managers treat employees this way?

As managers struggle to complete projects and keep their finger on the pulse of the organization, they show signs of frustration, which leads to impatience. *When bosses go wild* and impatience sets in, they tend to think employees are busy doing other things besides completing their assigned work. Side activities such as making personal calls, completing tasks requested by other departments, and taking extended lunches come to mind.

When employees miss project deadlines, skeptical bosses tend to treat everyone on the team, including those employees who met the due date, with the same negative vibe. These managers express the problem as a total team issue as if to suggest that everyone must pull their weight; otherwise, the project is destined for failure. This poor management style destroys morale as it makes employees believe that despite getting the job done, they cannot please their boss.

EMPLOYEE'S STRATEGY #1:
Consistently Produce at a High Level and Meet Deadlines.

Employee's Takeaway

Employees need to be aware that managers are under a great deal of pressure to produce on a consistent basis. Companies are constantly looking for opportunities to gain competitive advantages and differentiate themselves from competitors. With every passing day, the stress level rises throughout the company when goals are not met.

The best thing employees can do to deal with their skeptical boss is to continue to produce at a high level and consistently meet deadlines. Occasionally, try arriving to work earlier than your boss and put in some late nights from time-to-time. That will show your dedication and willingness to put in extra hours to accomplish team goals. Workers who consistently meet company and department objectives will, over time, earn the respect of management and eventually, even their skeptical boss.

It takes a special type of employee to take the emotion out of the situation and focus on the task at hand. When abrasive behavior and hurt feelings are tempered with patience, understanding, and hard work, it spawns appreciation. The next time your skeptical boss shows up at your desk, do not get frustrated; smile and say, "How can I support you today?"

MANAGER'S STRATEGY #1:
Create a Positive Work Environment for Employees.

Manager's Takeaway

Managers, you may be under pressure at

work to meet project deadlines; your boss may be on your back; and you may be dealing with personal issues at home. But none of these are valid reasons to create an unpleasant work environment for your staff. Treat your employees as business partners because, in reality, they are.

Your team deserves to be treated fairly and professionally. Making outlandish assumptions that employees "must be socializing instead of working" simply because they are not answering your call is unfounded. Asking employees to explain why your call went unanswered or making sarcastic remarks will negatively affect their morale. Trust in their positive intentions.

Employee's Commitment

In the space provided, determine your course of action the next time your boss responds in a manner that frustrates you. You can do it!

_____

_____

_____

Manager's Commitment

In the space provided, identify a suitable coaching style for the situation:

[Directing, Coaching, Facilitating, Delegating]

You can do it!

_____

_____

_____

Round 2: The Comparer

Problem

Similar to a good parent who pays careful attention not to liken one child to another, good bosses need to be reticent about comparing employees. Does your boss measure your performance with that of your co-workers? Do you feel that you are producing at a high level only to have your boss tell you that you need to do more? The answers to these questions and more may be found in subsequent sections.

Why do managers treat employees this way?

Bosses may not be aware of all of the moving pieces 'front-liners' like you have to deal with when working on a project. Although supervisors usually have a high-level understanding of projects, they seldom *sweat* the details. They can visualize how the puzzle should look once assembled, but struggle to fit all of the pieces together.

For example, multi-unit managers often make follow-up calls to their managers each week. At times, new processes are rolled-out through conference calls. If your area consists of 20 locations, for example, and your boss asks you to contact your team by the following week to ensure compliance, he will not ask about the complexities of completing the calls. Instead, he will expect the calls to be completed and the entire area to be trained by the go live date.

As the leader of the district, you are expected to get the job done without disrupting service. Even though you develop a plan and schedule your team's time at the beginning of the week, when it comes to conducting the calls, you find that many of your employees are busy servicing customers and cannot attend the calls. Sound familiar?

You end up rescheduling the meetings and move on to the next agenda item.

Although better planning could not have prevented this, bosses are seldom aware of the challenges employees face along the way. You may have completed the project by the deadline, but your peers may not have fared so well. As a result, your boss had to explain to the higher-ups why the region would not be 100% ready by the go live date.

When bosses go wild, they tend to respond irrationally to employees. Instead of pulling the one employee aside who caused the issue, they tend to take it out on the entire team.

You may have heard statements like, "Why can't we ever do things right?" Or, "Why does this keep happening?" Despite struggling to meet the deadline, your efforts are overlooked and you are compared to everyone else.

Employee's Takeaway

Keep your boss informed of the status of the project. Periodically, send an email or, better yet, call to let him know that you are experiencing hiccups along the way, but are managing through it and will meet the deadline. That will accomplish two things: 1) it will show your boss that you are sensitive to business needs and are capable of making situational decisions on your own; and 2) it will show your boss that you see him as a business partner by seeking his advice when needed.

MANAGER'S STRATEGY #2:
Treat Each Employee Like an Individual.

Manager's Takeaway

Do not compare team member performance. If you do not have the facts, stop and ask questions. It is not fair to employees who are delivering consistently to be categorized with those who are not. Your staff looks to you for guidance, support, and leadership. When you speak in generalities and fail to recognize people who are striving to separate themselves from underperformers, it drives morale down.

Take your 'manager's hat' off and think about how you like to be led. Do you like to stand out or does being compared to your peers, who aren't on top of their business like you are sound motivating? If not, why are you treating your team like that? Show them that you are capable of recognizing good results when you see it. Your team deserves it and will appreciate you for it.

Employee's Commitment

In the space provided, determine your course of action the next time your boss responds in a manner that frustrates you. You can do it!

_____

_____

_____

Manager's Commitment

In the space provided, identify a suitable coaching style for the situation:

[Directing, Coaching, Facilitating, Delegating]

You can do it!

_____

_____

_____

Round 3: The Information Disseminator

Problem

Steinbeck wrote in *Of Mice and Men*, "The best-laid plans of mice and men often go awry." Although he was not referring to management or leadership, it can be applied in this space as well.

Managers who design strategies and employees lower down in the corporate hierarchy are expected to be on the same page when it comes to executing the vision, meeting key deliverables, and achieving targets by specified due dates. Projects often fail because the details do not get communicated to all of the people involved. Managers often have multiple projects going on concurrently. They have the challenging task of deploying their team: placing the right people on the right project at the right time is essential if the project is to be completed properly and when due.

Have you been assigned a project with limited information? Ever ask your supervisor for more direction only to get a blank stare in return? How about finishing a week-long project only to find that it was not close to what was needed?

Why do managers treat employees this way?

Throughout the year, companies identify key initiatives that are expected to help improve sales, workflows, or profits. It is fairly common to have a list of projects delegated to managers during planning meetings with not much more than a due date and key stakeholders to guide them. Although the requirements of a project are discussed at that time, the tactics of disseminating information to employees is left to individual managers.

Scenario: Monday morning, your boss walks in and assigns you a new project. You feel confident that you can get the job done, but ask if there are additional details. Your manager tells you that you know as much as he does and instructs you to get started.

A week passes and you email what you believe to be the completed project to your manager. Upon review, he tells you that it is nothing like what the company needed and that you should have asked for clarification if you did not understand the requirements. Sound familiar? He goes on to make you feel guilty by telling you that he only has a few days to redo it before he has to submit it to his boss.

When you remind him that you asked for clarity when the project was assigned, he tells you that he does not recall that conversation and that if you had asked for guidance, he would have stopped everything he was doing to help you.

Too often, managers have to rely on their staff to do the work on their behalf as they lack expertise in a given area. Bosses have the keen ability to visualize project outcomes but sometimes do not possess the technical skills necessary to complete the project on their own, or are too busy attending meetings to dedicate time to the project. This is where you, the Subject Matter Expert (SME), comes into play.

When information is inadequate to complete a project, it is typically caused by the manager's inability to communicate expectations clearly and comprehensively. Whether managers understand the details of the project at the time it is assigned to them is irrelevant. It is their responsibility to assign the work and see to it that the project is completed properly and when due.

EMPLOYEE'S STRATEGY #3:
Don't Take "No" For an Answer. Ask For Clarity.

Employee's Takeaway

Don't take "no" for an answer. If you don't have a clear understanding of what is being asked of you, seek clarity. The last time I checked, you were doing the work. If you do not know what is expected, how can you possibly complete the project?

Being the motivated and talented employee you are gives you a license to be a 'pebble-in-the-shoe' whenever you do not have enough information to do your job. After all, you hold yourself to a high standard; why not do the same with your boss? One of your manager's roles is to break down barriers. Lack of clarity sure sounds like an obstacle to me.

MANAGER'S STRATEGY #3:
Don't Assume Employees Understand. Set Clear Expectations.

Manager's Takeaway

Don't assume your workforce understands what you are looking for when you delegate work. Every assignment is unique and your guidance from the onset is essential if it is to be completed correctly. Employees grasp information differently. In the absence of clarity, the project is bound to be incomplete and will most assuredly have to be redone.

Holding team members accountable and turning in completed projects is easy; that is, if you have laid the groundwork for the project. Set clear expectations and follow-up with your team regularly to make sure their questions are answered.

Employee's Commitment

In the space provided, determine your course of action the next time your boss responds in a manner that frustrates you. You can do it!

_____

_____

_____

Manager's Commitment

In the space provided, identify a suitable coaching style for the situation:
[Directing, Coaching, Facilitating, Delegating] You can do it!

_____

_____

_____

Round 4: The Recognizer

Problem

Have you ever heard someone say, "You did a great job John." Normally, that would make you feel good right? Except your name is Mike. Sound familiar?

Good managers deflect the attention from themselves and let their subordinates receive accolades for a job well done. Successful leaders understand that their team's success ultimately translates to compliments for them from the 'higher-ups' in the company. It goes without saying that it is human nature to want to be liked and respected at work; however, managers need to know when to recognize the person who actually did the work.

Why do managers treat employees this way?

Insecure managers constantly need reassurance that they are doing a good job. They believe that they are the reason for the project's success despite not having done any of the work. In a study of entry-level and middle-managers, 38% stated that the project would not have been completed without their involvement. Did someone say "ego"?

That may be true at a supervisory level; however, at the line-level, nothing could be farther from the truth. In the absence of motivated and qualified SME's, projects could not be completed. Managers need to embrace that, although they are the center cog of the wheel, they are surrounded by intelligent and sturdy spokes who keep the work-wheel spinning.

EMPLOYEE'S STRATEGY #4:
Confront Your Boss. Don't Stand Quietly While They Are Praised For Your Work.

Employee's Takeaway

If your boss does not recognize you for something you did, confront him immediately.

Standing quietly in the background while he is praised for your efforts will most assuredly cause the act to be repeated. Although bosses may flippantly say that they "have your back," they really don't. Worker bees – open your eyes and do as Thomas Jefferson instructed his followers to do: "Do you want to know who you are? Don't ask. Act! Action will delineate and define you."

MANAGER'S STRATEGY #4:
Recognize Employees For a Job Well Done.

Manager's Takeaway

Recognize your employees for a job well done. They are working hard to help the organization succeed. Even if others do not know who completed the project, bring it up during your meeting. Deep down you know your team deserves the kudos [not you].

Try building Mike up and watch how he performs on his next project. Chances are now that he feels the gratification recognition brings, he's going to want more of it, which will continue to drive his performance. Never forget that verbal recognition is free, and it tends to infuse morale in even the most beaten down employee.

Morale is a powerful tool managers need to keep in their leadership toolbox. When morale is high, employees are willing to work longer hours, take on more work, and collaborate with others to ensure a successful project. Conversely, when morale is low, employees tend to do the bare minimum. They don't contribute ideas, they don't partner with others, and they definitely don't invest extra time in the project. Basically, they become clock-watchers like Fred Flintstone, who waited for 5 o'clock to slide down the dinosaur's tail to scamper home.

Employee's Commitment

In the space provided, determine your course of action the next time your boss responds in a manner that frustrates you. You can do it!

_____

_____

_____

Manager's Commitment

In the space provided, identify a suitable coaching style for the situation:

[Directing, Coaching, Facilitating, Delegating]

You can do it!

_____

_____

_____

Round 5: The Know It All

Problem

Have you ever been in a relationship in which the other person could do no wrong? Whether buying the wrong diapers or putting the sheets on backwards, everyone has an opinion.

Bosses have been known to have an opinion or two and are not bashful about expressing it. One of my *favorite* Boss-isms is,

"How's that college degree working for you"? I get it; they have an undeniably challenging and often dubious responsibility of getting work done through others, but do they have to be condescending while going about their business? Although managers are ultimately accountable for completing projects, they need to rely on the expertise of their employees to accomplish company goals.

Scenario: You walk into your supervisor's office to share the *great* idea you have about solving one of the organization's greatest problems: training. You have been thinking about it all weekend and are confident that he is going to love *your* plan. You pitch your idea and await his high five, but instead you hear,

"I have implemented many training programs in my 'past life' and I know what is needed." He goes on the say, "I'll tell you how you can help *me* when the time is right."

Let's break the boss's tepid response down to levels beyond scientific. If you believe that employees are self-motivated and want to be part of the solution as I do, you may also agree that they deserve to have a voice in the planning phase. Bringing them in after the plan has been identified to do the dirty work sends the wrong message. Motivated employees who do not feel like they have a voice are likely to lose interest over time and may even stop contributing ideas on process improvements and other company initiatives.

Why do managers treat employees this way?

Managers are zealots for solving problems. They have a tremendous responsibility resting on their shoulders, but sometimes allow their subconscious need to be right to cloud their judgment. This often leads to unpredictable responses to employee exuberance. Add to that organizational pressures to deliver consistent results and you have the makings of a *know it all* boss.

> ### EMPLOYEE'S STRATEGY #5:
> *Boldly Request To Have Your Ideas Heard.*

Employee's Takeaway

If you are passionate about something,

don't take "no" for an answer. Boldly request
to have your ideas heard. Walk into your
boss's office and proclaim that you have the
solution to the company's problem.

If you see that your supervisor is
dismissing your ideas, do as attorneys do in
times of inflection: when they have the facts,
they pound the facts. When they have the
law, they pound the law. When they have
neither, they pound the table.

Providing a laundry list of company issues
doesn't help anyone. Prove to your boss that
you are a team player and have the business
acumen to not only come up with actionable
ideas, but are capable of executing the plan
too. When opportunity knocks, you

better have your bags packed. After all, the value of a *BIG* idea lies in using it. It is the only way to earn a second chance.

MANAGER'S STRATEGY #5:

Give Employees a Voice. Allow Them To Be Part of the Solution.

Manager's Takeaway

Give your employees a voice and allow them to be part of the solution. Think about how hard it is to motivate employees who do not share the same goals as you. Now, look at the motivated employees on your team trying desperately to be heard. It is said that we should listen twice as much as we talk. After all, we were given two ears and only one mouth...get the point?

When there is a convergence of passion, talent, and an altruistic desire to contribute to the success of the organization, you have found a special employee. These team members, above all, need to be appreciated instead of being treated like underperforming workers merely out for a paycheck.

If you remove the passionate employee's voice and make him feel like a robot, he will begin looking for other employment opportunities. You think you have problems now; wait and see how your quality of life changes when your top-performer jumps ship. Sound ominous? It is. This grim reality could play itself out if you do not allow employee creativity to flow. In the end, you will receive the accolades. Treat those who truly care about the company as partners in your business. Do you want to do all the work yourself? If the answer is "heck no," then you need to act now.

Perhaps Edward R. Murrow said it best, "Just because your voice reaches halfway around the world doesn't mean you are wiser than when it reached only to the end of the bar." Management translation: just because you are in a position of power does not mean you have all the answers. Consult with your team as often as possible.

"A fool's mouth is his destruction, and his lips are the snare of his soul."

—Proverbs 18:7

Employee's Commitment

In the space provided, determine your course of action the next time your boss responds in a manner that frustrates you. You can do it!

_____

_____

_____

Manager's Commitment

In the space provided, identify a suitable coaching style for the situation: [Directing, Coaching, Facilitating, Delegating] You can do it!

_____

_____

_____

Round 6: The Late Night Worker

Problem

Are you kidding me? Another midnight email from my boss while I was asleep? If you are anything like me, you cannot help but wonder whether your boss is overly-committed to the job or should be committed to the Graybar Motel? (No offense to the asylums across the country). Studies have shown that not sleeping enough takes years off of our lives. Despite this factoid, high-level supervisors continue to do laps around their employees in the *commitment* pool.

When managers continue to work hours after their employees have gone home for the day, are they trying to role model the behavior they expect team members to emulate? Or, are they so inefficient during the day that the only time they can get their work done is after everyone has left the building?

When supervisors expect employees to work longer hours than normal, is it justified? If you are able to work a nine-hour day, while eating lunch at your desk to be able to leave an hour earlier than others who went out to lunch, should that be frowned upon by your boss? I say, "Absolutely not!"

Why do managers treat employees this way?

Working late to finish a job is admirable; however, taking eight hours to finish a project that should have taken half that time could indicate one of two things: either the manager attends too many meetings, or he does not know how to allocate the scarcest of management resources, time.

Productivity is a measure of the efficiency of production and it is gauged in various ways: hours worked, tasks completed, and time per unit produced. Depending on who you ask, the answer may be different. It is silly to expect the workforce to arrive and leave at the same time each day. However, when an employee leaves earlier than others, some managers cannot help but ask, "Why can't you be as committed as [insert name of co-worker]."

EMPLOYEE'S STRATEGY #6:
Do Not Give Into Unreasonable Inferences.

Employee's Takeaway

Don't feel like you have to change your work hours because your boss *suggested* you do so. Provided you are putting in your time and producing at a high-level, do not give in.

Do the math. You get to work at 8 o'clock in the morning and leave at 5 o'clock. You eat lunch at your desk on most days so that you can continue working on your projects. Any way you slice it, it equates to a nine-hour day.

Conversely, your co-worker strolls in at 9-ish, takes an hour lunch, and leaves at 7-ish. To the rationale thinker, that still works out to be a nine-hour work day. However, to some managers and certainly the person working until 7 o'clock, it seems as though he is more committed. Can someone explain how that possibly makes sense?

MANAGER'S STRATEGY #6:
Don't Stifle an Employee's Work Ethic.

Manager's Takeaway

Don't stifle an employee's work ethic. By fawning over late-night workers simply because they are working as late as you, you are destroying the morale of other team members. Like many high-priced products produced today are not always the best quality, so too is work produced after-hours. Before responding to a situation, make sure you have the details straight. Do a quick calculation of hours worked and projects completed. If one of your workers comes in at a higher productivity rate than another, celebrate their success. If you see him eating at his desk so he can leave on time each day to spend more time with his family, be compassionate and respect him for doing so. Do not berate him, and do not compare him to others. That will only create friction between the two of you.

Occasionally, thank your employees for a job well done. Trust me; by doing so, you will improve their morale and enrich their job. You owe it to your hard-working employees to treat them like individuals who are pulling and pushing in the same direction as you.

Employee's Commitment

In the space provided, determine your course of action the next time your boss responds in a manner that frustrates you. You can do it!

_____

_____

_____

Manager's Commitment

In the space provided, identify a suitable coaching style for the situation:

[Directing, Coaching, Facilitating, Delegating]

You can do it!

_____

_____

_____

Round 7: The Over-Committer

Problem

Ever hear your boss say, "So much to do and so little time to do it"? If not, be patient; it's coming. Bosses are the consummate over-committers. They go into a meeting with their peers and come out with more projects. The funny thing is, at times, they volunteer for the extra work. Here is how it all shakes out: someone in the room brings up a department challenge that they are struggling with, and usually, one of their peers makes a suggestion to get them over the hump. When that does not seem to work, the 'leader of the pack' will ask for another department head to partner with the struggling manager. Invariably, someone in the room will volunteer to help.

Normally, I encourage people to offer assistance to anyone in need of help, except when the person volunteering has no business signing up his team for another department's project. To add value to the project, the contributor needs to have an idea of how to get it off the ground; otherwise, it is going to be a waste of time and the product will not be of any value.

To illustrate this point, imagine being on the Purchasing Team and being asked to work on a project with Information Technology (IT). I know exactly what you are thinking; the extent of your IT knowledge is turning on your computer and logging on, right? Keep smiling; it gets better.

Why do managers treat employees this way?

If your manager is anything like mine, he enjoys being the one-stop-shop for all of the organization's needs. Although he will never admit this, he believes that he needs to stand out in the crowd so that his supervisor sees him as someone that can be counted on in tough times. Whether the problem is training, sales, or distribution-related, if the company believes that John can do it because he has come through in the past, guess who gets assigned the extra work?

Sure, John can resist a few times, using up credits he has accrued for helping his boss out of a bind in the past, but how many times can he get away with that before his boss starts second-guessing his work ethic or commitment? Think about it like this, when you are up for a promotion and are offered a job that you really do not want, you can turn it down. In fact, you may decide to do the same on the next opportunity too. If, however, you have not accepted an offer by the third or certainly the fourth time opportunity knocks, the opportunity fountain eventually dries out, and you are left to wonder why the company no longer respects your work.

EMPLOYEE'S STRATEGY #7:
If You Enjoy the Fruits of Your Labor,
Don't Complain About the Labor.

Employee's Takeaway

If you enjoy the fruits of your labor, don't complain about the labor. Look at the extra work your boss is assigning you as a privilege. Instead of giving it to someone else on the team, he asked you to do it, which should give your confidence and ego a boost. These types of opportunities are outstanding ways to make in-roads with other department heads with whom you have limited exposure.

As more job advancement opportunities become available in your company, if another manager is familiar with your work because of the project you worked on together, that may be the edge you need to get the promotion.

Aside from helping others for the sheer joy of contributing to your organization's success, you should also look at it as a growth opportunity for yourself. While many people attend seminars to develop their skillset, when you are given an opportunity to pick up additional knowledge in an area that you are not normally exposed to and, on the company's dime, carpe diem. Interested? Keep reading.

When the economy contracts and companies are forced to reduce their workforce, you do not want to be on the short list of people being let go. Instead, focus on becoming your team's utility player, with ubiquitous talents.

MANAGER'S STRATEGY #7:
Be a Valuable Resource For Your Company.

Manager's Takeaway

Continue being a reliable resource for your company—it is much appreciated! Although your employees may not understand why you are taking on extra work, as long as you are doing it for the right reasons, keep it up. Times are tough and companies need people like you to step in and solve problems.

Don't sign up for projects for the sake of getting your name on the cover page. If you are not doing it for the right reasons, then stand down and wait for the next opportunity. If, however, you feel compelled to help and know your Team can contribute at a high level, what are you waiting for? Roll up your sleeves and help.

Employee's Commitment

In the space provided, determine your course of action the next time your boss responds in a manner that frustrates you. You can do it!

_____

_____

_____

Manager's Commitment

In the space provided, identify a suitable coaching style for the situation:

[Directing, Coaching, Facilitating, Delegating]

You can do it!

_____

_____

_____

Round 8: The Credit Snatcher

Problem

It is often said that there is no "I" in
Team. There is, however, a "me"—and Bosses
know it. As projects are completed, the person
doing the work should receive the credit,
right? Sometimes reality does not follow logic,
especially if you are working for a predatory
boss.

In a study of working college students,
47% said their boss had taken credit for their

work without as much as a mention of their name during a management team meeting. The respondents went on to say that not receiving credit for their work would not have been so bad if their boss had not swooped in like a ravenous vulture to steal the spotlight. In the same study, 29% of respondents pointed to this management shortcoming as the insurmountable concern that would make them want to quit their job. The feeling was that, if managers could nonchalantly put their name on someone else's work, what else were they capable of taking from their employees? Morale? Work-life balance? Promotional opportunities?

Recognition is an inexpensive way for companies to make employees feel good about their performance. When employees spend more time at work than they do with their families, they are not doing so for their health. Some do it for the money; others do it for the gratification of helping others, and another segment of the population does it for the sheer joy a pat-on-the-back brings them.

Why do managers treat employees this way?

Insecurity makes people do things they would not normally do at work. When managers are not confident in their own ability, but have a top-notch employee on their team who consistently produces quality work, they are likely to take the credit away from the employee to make themselves look good.

It is not uncommon for these types of managers to make people think that they did the analysis that saved the company hundreds of thousands of dollars, or improved the work flow that increased productivity, which allowed the company to operate with fewer employees.

EMPLOYEE'S STRATEGY #8:
Take Credit For Your Work.

Employee's Takeaway

If you did the work, take credit for it. Although you may not receive an 'ata boy' for a particular project, when you string enough of these achievements together, one of two things will happen: either your name will forever be linked with successful projects you took part in; or others will know that your manager is the one hiding behind the curtain taking your credit—Either way, you win!

Be diplomatic about informing others of your involvement in a project. After all, you don't want people to start thinking of you in the same way you feel about your boss. If you did the work, take the credit. Similarly, if you were part of the team that completed the project, mention your involvement, but be careful about stealing your team's glory. Maintain your humility and recognize the

Manager's Commitment

In the space provided, identify a suitable coaching style for the situation:

[Directing, Coaching, Facilitating, Delegating]

You can do it!

_____

_____

_____

Round 9: The "Over" Talker

Problem

Have you ever hosted a conference call with your boss in the room with you? *You* call the meeting; *you* invite attendees, and *you* create the agenda. But, when it comes to conducting the call, you struggle to get a word in edgewise because your boss dominates the discussion. Sound familiar?

Why do managers treat employees this way?

Generally, managers are talented, hard-working, and strategic thinkers who help their teams navigate through a laundry list of to-dos each day. Conversely, other managers have been known to be opinionated, self-serving and unwilling to let subordinates lead in their presence.

At the end of the day, managers own their projects and go about getting work done using their dominant leadership style. Some managers are comfortable **delegating**, while others take a more **facilitative** approach to leading their team. These two styles are better for employee morale in that it affords managers a more hands-off approach and allows employees to use their creativity to complete their work. These styles, however, require employees to be highly motivated and capable of completing projects with little or no supervision. On the other hand, other managers feel more comfortable **supporting** or **directing** the activities of team members due to their team's low motivation and ability.

Although successful managers can interweave the four coaching styles into their interactions with employees, all leaders have a dominant style they rely on when they feel things are spiraling out of control.

Employee's Takeaway

How many more meetings are you going to let your boss dominate the discussion? If your boss is talking over you during your own meeting, it may indicate a lack of trust. You need to put an end to this disrespect immediately. I recommend going off-site, perhaps to a local coffee house or restaurant to have a heart-to-heart discussion about your feelings.

Get to the root of the problem. The last thing you want is for your boss to dominate yet another conversation and justify his management style. Instead, focus on the solution. Let him know that you are capable of conducting meetings on your own and would rather have him take on a consulting role rather than talking over you.

MANAGER'S STRATEGY #9:

Trust Your Employees. Empower Them So They Can Do Their Job.

Manager's Takeaway

Even a broken clock is right twice a day. Unless your employee's status has changed, thus bringing their work ethic or ability into question, let them do the job they were hired to do. Don't be a *know it all* by interjecting your opinions and 'best laid plans' into the conversation just because you outrank the presenter. Remember, you are an invited guest. Conduct yourself accordingly.

If, on the other hand, there is a bona fide reason to second-guess your employee's ability to conduct the call, you should address the issue in private. You are doing him a disservice by letting him think he is leading the call, especially when you had other plans.

By talking over your employee, you are destroying his morale and sending him negative vibes about your level of trust and confidence in him. If you do not change your behavior, over time, your employees will stop taking the initiative to solve problems on their own and will start deferring to you to make all of the decisions. Is that what you really want? If not, empower them.

Employee's Commitment

In the space provided, determine your course of action the next time your boss responds in a manner that frustrates you. You can do it!

_____

_____

_____

Manager's Commitment

In the space provided, identify a suitable coaching style for the situation:

[Directing, Coaching, Facilitating, Delegating]

You can do it!

_____

_____

_____

Round 10: The Executor

Problem

Talented managers have an uncanny knack of putting strategies in place to help the company achieve its goals. Strategies, however, are only as good as the team's ability to execute the plan. Good strategies also fail and, when that happens, it is often more difficult to pinpoint the reasons for the breakdown. Despite the obvious need for good planning and execution, few managers seem to focus on the processes and leadership styles that will translate strategies into results.

While execution can be affected by a variety of factors, one of the most basic shortcomings is allowing the focus of the team to shift over time. Focusing on such things as pricing integrity one week, service the next, and expense controls soon thereafter causes confusion within the department and contributes to the strategy short-fall.

Have you ever been rushed to complete a project only to hear that the "key initiative" your boss talked about for weeks is no longer an organizational focus? Ever hear your boss say, "Timing is everything"? While following-up is a management tenet, when employees do not see their hard work put into motion, over time it sends them a message that their time and work is not valued. Furthermore, when the 'hurry-up and wait' philosophy permeates throughout the organization, morale is negatively impacted and employees lose interest in working on their projects.

Why do managers treat employees this way?

Managers like to be the first to the party. When their supervisor asks about the status of a project, they want to come from a position of strength, which is loosely translated as, "I finished my project before my peers."

Managers like checking things off of their list of things to do. They are tacticians who are great at putting tasks into motion and following-up to make sure team members are working towards achieving department goals.

> ## EMPLOYEE'S STRATEGY #10:
> *Push Back on Work When You Are 'Maxed' Out.*
>
> *Remind Your Boss That You Are Working on Multiple Projects.*

Employee's Takeaway

Our parents taught us that, "If we don't have anything nice to say, we shouldn't say anything at all." That does not apply when you are doing all the work. Stand up for yourself and let your boss know that you have already been assigned multiple projects this month. There are only so many hours in a day, and if you expect to produce your usual top-quality work, you need to push back—hard.

Your boss is going to try to entice you with a few 'old school' motivational techniques. You can expect to be taken to lunch, receive a special delivery of your favorite premium coffee, or hear how much the company values your work. After reading this, you now know what to do, right? Accept the trinkets and then vehemently push back. Those tactics are part of a manager's ruse to get you to stay committed to a project...or, in this case, projects.

Manager's Takeaway

Recognize that employees have a productivity ceiling. While motivated workers will do whatever it takes to help the team succeed, dumping more work on them when they have not completed any of the previously assigned projects is a mistake. It will negatively affect their morale, cause them to spread themselves too thin, and perhaps more of a concern for managers, it will cause them to take shortcuts to get the projects off of their desk. In the end, it is sure to cause dissension between the manager and the employee.

Cap your project list at three deliverables at any one time. When a project is completed, check it off and add another one from your project repository. Let's face it; there will never be a shortage of projects. But that does not mean that you should forget how it felt to be a Worker Bee when you were coming up the ranks.

Employee's Commitment

In the space provided, determine your course of action the next time your boss responds in a manner that frustrates you. You can do it!

_____

_____

_____

Manager's Commitment

In the space provided, identify a suitable coaching style for the situation:

[Directing, Coaching, Facilitating, Delegating]

You can do it!

_____

_____

_____

Round 11:

Talking Out of Both Sides of Your Mouth

Problem

Have you ever been accused of being a clerk when your true title was analyst? Has the same boss asked you to order lunch for an upcoming meeting after chastising you for not being committed to your project list?

In a study of working adults, 25% of respondents stated that they had experienced such fickle folly, and that it would be the number one reason for them seeking other employment opportunities.

This management characteristic may be the most frustrating of them all as you really never know which side of his mouth your boss will be speaking to you next. He may tell you to take ownership of your projects, but ends up micro-managing every move you make. How does that make sense? Believe me, it happens, and when it does, that feeling you get in the pit of your stomach will be the bartender's latest drink called frustration.

Why do managers treat employees this way?

Although your manager may have been in your position when he was coming up the ranks, his awareness of what you go through on a daily basis has changed. Given the limited resources managers often work with, they sometimes have to compensate for their lack of expertise by saying one thing even though they mean another.

Here is an exchange between a supervisor and his employee: [Supervisor] "You need to be more productive." Minutes later, the employee's phone rings. [Supervisor] "I have been trying to reach Bill, but he's not answering his phone. Please look for him in the building and ask him to call my cell phone."

These conflicting exchanges often cause confusion and resentment for employees. Imagine being instructed to do your job and then something completely unrelated. No big deal right? What if the person you were asked to "track down" didn't work on the same floor as you? Would you be less willing to search for Bill if he worked two floors beneath you?

EMPLOYEE'S STRATEGY #11:
Ask Your Boss To Stop Sending Mixed Messages.

Employee's Takeaway

This is a delicate situation that requires careful action. On one hand, you need to ask your boss to stop sending you mixed messages. Make him aware that it is causing you frustration and confusion. On the other hand, you are an employee and, technically, can be asked to do anything (within the law) your boss needs.

The last thing you want is to disrupt any semblance of chemistry that exists between the two of you. After all, you don't know the pressure he is under at the moment.
By ordering lunch or finding Bill, it will relieve your manager's stress and make you an instant hero in his eyes.

Manager's Takeaway

Respect your employees' time. Be cognizant of their project load and the strict deadlines that come with it. According to a study conducted by the Airline industry, it takes 25 minutes for employees to regain their focus after an office interruption. Moreover, the study went on to say that office workers typically only go 11 minutes without being interrupted.

It is one thing to utilize your resources, but another to ask your employees to do things your boss would never ask you to do. If their job description does not include ordering lunch, you may want to order it yourself to avoid striking a morale chord. The last thing you need is to destroy team member morale, especially of those employees who truly have your back.

Treat employees with the same respect and professionalism you expect from your boss. Employees are more productive with positive reinforcement. Give it a try. You won't be disappointed.

Employee's Commitment

In the space provided, determine your course of action the next time your boss responds in a manner that frustrates you. You can do it!

_____

_____

_____

Manager's Commitment

In the space provided, identify a suitable coaching style for the situation:

[Directing, Coaching, Facilitating, Delegating]

You can do it!

_____

_____

_____

Round 12: The Conclusion Jumper

Problem

If there was a mirror in your room that made you look four feet tall and two feet wide, over the years, would you believe that was how you really looked? Let's see if we can put a management spin on this. Managers are notorious for being creatures of habit. If something worked for them 20 years ago, it will most assuredly work for them today.

Similarly, if they dealt with an employee issue years ago and their current employee is demonstrating similar behaviors, they are likely to form the same conclusions.

Although the players change over time, the outcome remains the same [at least that is what they believe]. What managers fail to realize is that if the leader, the follower, and the situation are not aligned, their best coaching efforts will be ineffective.

The training program from 20 years ago that the team spent three years developing and another two years testing may have worked then, but the players and situation may be different today and, thus, may lead to a different outcome.

Have you been on a business call and the conversation turned personal because you had developed a good working relationship with the other person throughout the years? What if your boss walked in just as you were asking Jim about the health of his son who was recently in the hospital?

Here's another example to consider: if you were speaking with your wife about an important decision that had to be made by 5 o'clock that evening, and it could not wait until you got home, would your manager jump to the conclusion that all of your conversations, especially when he was not in the office, were of a personal nature?

Why do managers treat employees this way?

Some managers don't care about cause and effect. They have already made up their mind with the limited information they have, and no one is going to change it. Experience is an effective and powerful tool for managers to carry. If not used properly, it can lead to mismanagement and poor utilization of resources.

When employees are instructed to do something because the manager knows how all the moving pieces fit together, there may be a missed opportunity by not asking for the team's input.

Employee's Takeaway

It is very frustrating working for a *conclusion jumper.* You know how hard you work and the lengths you go to avoid taking personal calls at work. After working together so long, you expect your boss to know you better than that by now.

Nothing you say is going to change your manager's perception of you. Every time the phone rings and your boss is in the room with you, guess what he is thinking?

Go about your business and do not worry about things you can't control. *WOW them instead of WHY them*! Stop asking yourself why you are being treated that way. Success comes from turning problems into opportunities, and you should be thinking of the present opportunity as an investment instead of an expense. WOW your boss and co-workers with your positive attitude and strong work ethic.

Do not change your communication style as that is what makes you special and so endearing to others. Your personalized approach to problem solving is refreshing especially when the caller is at his wits end and needs help. Asking about the caller's family, for example, brings a level of calm to the situation that is much appreciated and sets you apart from others.

> ## *MANAGER'S STRATEGY #12:*
> *Be Proud of Your Employees.*
>
> *Don't Try To Change Something That Isn't Broken.*

Manager's Takeaway

Remember how it felt when you received a gift when you were young? If you were anything like me, you shook the box and perhaps smelled it to determine what was inside. In the end, you tore the wrapping paper off with reckless abandon to see your surprise.

Although managers are taught to *think outside the box* early in their career, I encourage you to think *inside* the box to see the value your employees bring to your department. The work environment (inside) is comprised of hard-working employees who want to do a good job; so why not treat them with the same respect that you expect from your boss.

You should be proud of your employees for personalizing conversations especially given the stress that exists at work today. As long as your employee is completing projects by the deadline and does so with a positive attitude, don't try to change something that's not broken.

It is difficult enough finding employees who genuinely care about what they do, but if you are lucky enough to find one that also cares about the happiness of others, leverage it. You have a unique and valuable individual whose talents should be embraced and encouraged. Stop the scoffing and sarcasm. It is destroying team member morale.

Employee's Commitment

In the space provided, determine your course of action the next time your boss responds in a manner that frustrates you. You can do it!

_____

_____

_____

Manager's Commitment

In the space provided, identify a suitable coaching style for the situation:

[Directing, Coaching, Facilitating, Delegating]

You can do it!

_____

_____

_____

Conclusion

I may not be able to define good management, but I know it when I see it. Times change, but basic management principles remain the same. Management style greatly affects employee motivation and their capacity to learn. Talented managers utilize the appropriate coaching technique based on an employee's motivation, ability, time constraints, and project load.

For coaching to be effective, the leader, the follower, and the situation must all be aligned. Although there is not a 'best-in-class' management style that can be applied unilaterally to all situations, leaning too heavily on any one style will eventually lead to ineffective management. Effective leaders use a variety of techniques, and they know how and when to choose the most appropriate style for the given situation.

Unfortunately, some managers fail to utilize different management styles, either because they do not know how or they do not see the value in changing from their dominant style.

Good bosses care about getting things done. Exceptional bosses care about their people. Good bosses have strong organizational skills and have the ability to make solid decisions. Good bosses get important things done.

Exceptional bosses do all of the above—and more. Sure, they care about their company and customers, their vendors and suppliers. But most importantly, they care to an exceptional degree about the people who work for them.

Exceptional bosses make it incredibly easy for employees to offer suggestions. They help employees feel comfortable proposing new ways to get things done. When an idea isn't feasible, they always take the time to explain why.

Exceptional bosses know that employees who make suggestions care about the company and they ensure that those employees know their input is valued—and appreciated.

Along the road to perfection, exceptional bosses find excellence. They change the everyday into the epic; the mundane into the monumental.

Every employee works for a paycheck, but employees want more from their job than a paycheck: They want to work with and for people they respect and admire—and with and for people who respect and admire them.

That's why a kind word, a quick discussion about family, and an informal conversation to ask if an employee needs help are much more important than group meetings or formal evaluations. A true sense of connection is personal, which is why exceptional bosses show that they see and appreciate the person, not just the worker.

John F. Kennedy once declared that, "We are not their rivals for power, but partners for progress." That reference is deep-rooted in management annals and is further delineated by encouraging managers to partner with employees to achieve company goals.

The words managers speak to employees are powerful. They can either destroy an employee's morale or build him up. A word to all the managers out there: care for your employees' well-being. In some cases, you may be the only person in their lives to speak words of encouragement to them. Choose your words wisely and make them count.

Least Liked Supervisory Traits That Would Cause Employees To Quit Their Job.

Credit Snatcher	29%
Talking Out of Both Sides of Your Mouth	25%
Conclusion Jumper	10%
Know It All	8%
Over Talker	8%
Skeptic	8%
Information Disseminator	8%
Recognizer	4%
Late Night Worker	2%
Comparer	0%
Over Committer	0%
Executor	0%

The data above is taken from an independent study the author conducted over the span of a year. Working students between the ages of 21 – 50 were asked to rank supervisory traits in order of the ones they liked least. The percentages indicate how many workers would quit their job if their boss goes wild.

About the Author

Eddie Loussararian received his Bachelor of Science (BS) degree from Cal Poly Pomona where he studied Hotel and Restaurant Management. Several years after gaining valuable work experience, he obtained his Master of Business Administration (MBA) degree from the University of Redlands.

Since graduating from school, Mr. Loussararian has held many challenging and rewarding positions for a pair of Fortune 100 companies. After seven years in the restaurant industry, he was recruited by a leading hotel company, where he transitioned as a Regional Manager.

With a passion for reporting and analytics, as well as an insatiable desire to develop training programs to help companies improve operational workflows and operating margins, he strayed far from the hospitality industry and went to work for the nation's leader in the flooring industry as an Internal Audit Manager.

Since then, as a college instructor, coach, corporate trainer, and facilitator, he has successfully applied the management concepts described in this manuscript in a variety of settings.

Mr. Loussararian has been married to his wife, Michelle, for seventeen years, and they have a son and two daughters. He lives in Los Angeles County.

"Do you want to know who you are? Don't ask. Act! Action will delineate and define you."

—Thomas Jefferson

Made in the USA
San Bernardino, CA
22 April 2016